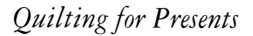

Quilting for Presents

Quilting for Presents

Wendy Jackson

Webb&Bower
EXETER, ENGLAND

First published in Great Britain 1986 by
Webb & Bower (Publishers) Limited
9 Colleton Crescent, Exeter, Devon EX2 4BY

Edited, designed and illustrated by
E.T. Archive Ltd, 9 Chelsea Wharf, 15 Lots Road
London SW10 0QH

Designed by Julian Holland
Photography by Eileen Tweedy
Drawings and charts by Cedric Robson
Painted furniture lent by Dragons of Walton Street Ltd
Production by Nick Facer

British Library Cataloguing in Publication Data
Jackson, Wendy
    Quilting for presents. — (Crafts for presents; 4)
    1. Quilting
    I. Title   II. Series
    746.46   TT835

    ISBN 0–86350–093–5

Phototypeset by Tradespools Ltd, Frome, Somerset

Printed and bound in Hong Kong
by Mandarin Offset Marketing (HK) Ltd.

Contents

Introduction

Although it is difficult to trace the origins of quilting, the idea of stitching together three layers of fabric in a pattern for warmth and decoration has been around for hundreds of years. Quilting has been fashionable for clothes right up to the present day, but in this book I have tried to show a variety of other projects where quilting can be used. In some cases patchwork and appliqué are used as well, since these combine so well with quilting.

I hope that you will get double pleasure from this book. First of all in making the projects, and secondly in giving them and in your friends receiving them. I am sure that you will have many more ideas of your own and will perhaps want to adapt some of those shown here. But whatever the case, I hope you will find, as I do, that quilting in all its forms is a very relaxing and satisfying aspect of needlework. Some of the projects are fairly quick and simple to make, but I have also included several that require a little more skill and patience.

As the metric and imperial measurements are not always exact equivalents, choose one or the other and keep to it for the duration of that project. In instances where only small pieces of fabric are required, no measurements have been given.

Types of quilting

Wadded (English) quilting

This is the oldest form of quilting and consists of three layers, the top fabric, the wadding and the backing fabric. Light- or medium-weight natural fibres such as silk, satin and cotton give the best results, although it is always worth experimenting with other materials. There are many different kinds of waddings on the market, but for all the projects in this book polyester wadding has been used. As well as being easily available by the metre, it is also washable and comes in different thicknesses. Never iron synthetic waddings.

The backing fabrics most suitable for quilting are calico, curtain-lining or even old sheeting, but any firm fabric will do. The threads used should match the top fabric and a buttonhole twist thread or similar gives a bolder stitching line than ordinary sewing cotton. Generally try to use silk on silk and cotton on cotton etc. The needles used are crewel or sharps.

Always press fabrics before starting work, as this cannot be done when the work is completed.

It is always advisable to work quilting in a frame (see page 8) as this prevents puckering and distortion. Both hands are then left free for quilting, which should be done in a single, stabbing, vertical movement. Quilting done on the machine, however, can be worked without a frame using the ordinary presser foot. Remember here always to work rows in the same direction to prevent distorting the fabric.

Before mounting the backing fabric on to the frame, make sure that the fabric is cut on the grain in both directions and match the centre of the backing fabric to the centre of the frame. The backing fabric is then stretched on to a frame using drawing pins or a staple gun at regular intervals.

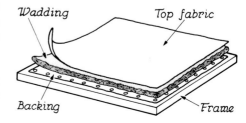

Wadding *Top fabric*

Backing *Frame*

The wadding is then laid over the backing and finally the top fabric upon which the design has already been transferred. All three layers are then tacked together and it is very important that this stage is done thoroughly to prevent the fabric from slipping while working.

For small pieces of work tack the layers of fabric together out from the centre (diagram A), but on larger pieces, work in horizontal and vertical rows, about 5 cm (2 in) apart, from the centre outwards in each case, smoothing the fabric while stitching (diagram B).

the design, making sure all the shapes are enclosed, using running or back stitch. Remove the tackings and then turn the work over to the wrong side. Make a small slit through the backing fabric only, in the centre of the design and, using acrylic filling, insert small pieces at a time using a knitting needle or crochet hook. Make sure that any points are well filled. Do not push too much padding in at a time or there will be a lumpy effect, and do not use cotton wool as a filling material for the same reason. Continue stuffing until there is a nicely raised shape on the front. Stitch up the slit.

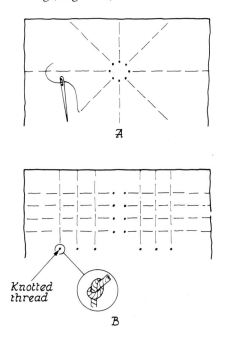

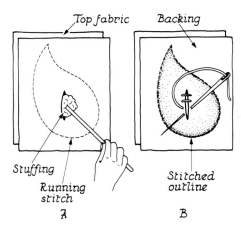

Small pieces of *trapunto* quilting may be completed in a hoop or tambour frame if well tacked beforehand and if the complete design fits within the frame.

Stuffed (trapunto) quilting

This consists of two layers of fabric. The top fabric which can be any closely woven, light- or medium-weight fabric, such as that used for wadded quilting, and a backing fabric such as calico or old sheeting. Transfer the design to the top fabric and place on top of the backing fabric. Tack together well and then stitch round

Corded (Italian) quilting

Corded quilting like stuffed quilting, uses only two layers of fabric. A top fabric which can be any smooth, closely woven material and a backing fabric. The design is achieved by stitching parallel lines through the two layers to make a channel. Place the top fabric on top of the backing fabric, having first transferred the design, making sure that all the lines are double. Tack together securely. Stitch, using running or back stitch. Remove the tacking threads. Using a quilting wool or any thread that will fill the space between the lines of stitching, thread a tapestry needle and insert the wool between the layers of fabric, making sure that the top fabric is not pierced. At any points or sharp curves, bring the needle out through the backing and re-insert it through the same hole, leaving the small loop of wool showing on the backing. Trim the ends of the quilting wool to about 3 mm ($\frac{1}{8}$ in).

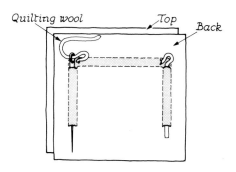

Quilting wool   Top   Back

Stitches

The stitches generally used for quilting are running or back stitch, but any line stitch could be experimented with. The size of the stitches is not too important, but aim to get them as even as possible. Do not pull them too tightly or they will pucker the quilting.

Back stitch will make a definite quilting line. Working from right to left bring the needle out on the line from the underside of the fabric and make a short straight stitch to the right. Take the needle back down and bring it out to the left, following the line. Re-insert the needle into the same hole as the previous stitch and repeat along the line.

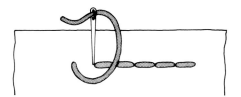

Running stitch was the traditional stitch used on quilts. It makes a less definite line than back stitch, but if carefully worked can be reversible.

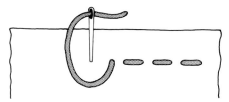

Look for other line stitches that could be used for quilting. To secure the thread, start with a tiny back stitch into the backing fabric and finish off by darning the thread into the back of the work. Remove all the tacking threads when the quilting is finished. Remember also to allow for shrinkage when quilting, especially on clothing or large items.

Frames

Although much embroidery can be worked without a frame, quilting is one of the areas where it is very necessary. Although there are special quilting frames, I prefer to use a simple home-made wooden one consisting of four pieces of wood joined together with brackets.

Alternatively, an artist stretcher or even an old picture frame could be used. The fabric is secured with drawing pins or, if available, a staple gun. I would only use a hoop or tambour frame for small pieces of *trapunto* or Italian quilting where the whole design fits within the frame.

Enlarging a design

As most of the designs in this book are shown smaller than they actually are, it will be necessary to enlarge them. The same method can then be applied to any photograph or drawing which you may want to enlarge. Start by placing a piece of tracing paper over the original drawing and tracing the design with a pencil. Draw a rectangle around it and divide it into equal squares—2.5 cm (1 in) for a fairly simple design, but 1 cm (½ in) would be needed for a more complicated design. Following the diagram, number and letter the squares. Place the traced design in the bottom left-hand corner of a large piece of paper and draw a line along the bottom edge of the paper—the required width of the design. Draw a diagonal line from the bottom left-hand corner to the height required. Complete the rectangle by drawing in the new sides.

Divide the new rectangle into the same number of squares as in the original.

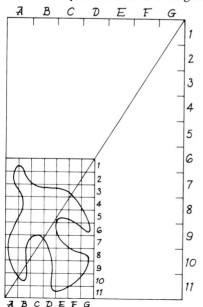

Number and letter them as before. Now the lines can be drawn in from the small squares to the large one. This method can equally be applied for reducing a design.

Transferring designs

Once the design has been enlarged to the correct size, it can be transferred to the fabric and this should generally be done before it is framed up.

Scratch marking

This is the method traditionally used for English quilting. The template is laid in position on the fabric and a needle pressed firmly all round the outline. This lightly scratches the surface and leaves a mark which will last long enough to work the quilting. This method is really only suitable for natural fabrics as the fibres on man-made materials tend to spring back when scratched.

Tracing

This method can be used on most light- and medium-weight fabrics, such as cotton, lawn, satin, calico, silk etc. Draw the design on to white paper with a black felt-tip pen. Place the design on to a light-coloured flat surface and place the material on top of this. Secure with masking tape. Trace the outline through with a water-soluble marking pen. Alternatively, use a fine paintbrush and watercolour paint. If you wish to use this method but cannot quite make out the design through the fabric, try taping it to a window, so that the light shines through and then trace in the design.

Tracing and tacking

For fabrics where the tracing method is unsuitable, particularly textured fabrics, trace the design on to a piece of tissue-paper and place it on the right side of the material. Pin the paper to the fabric at the edges and using a thread which will show up on the fabric, tack around all the lines of the design through both the fabric and paper using tiny running stitches on all curves to keep the shape. Make sure that the ends are secured thoroughly. Remove the pins and gently tear off the tissue-paper, leaving the design marked out on the fabric. Remove the tacking stitches as the quilting is worked.

Making up piped cushions

Piping cord is available in a variety of thicknesses, so buy one that is in proportion to the cushion being made. Remember to wash the cord before use as it can shrink and would spoil a lot of hard work. Cut on the cross a number of strips of fabric about 4 cm (1½ in) wide.

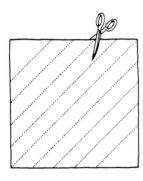

Join these pieces of fabric where necessary on the straight grain.

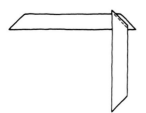

Fold the fabric right side outwards round the cord and stitch close to the cord. Tack the covered piping cord to the right side of the front of the cushion with all the raw edges together. Machine stitch all the way round. Snip into the corners almost up to the piping.

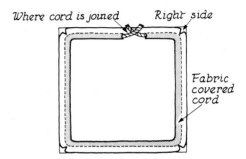

To join the piping, trim the two ends of the cord so that there is about 2 cm (1 in) overlap. Unravel the two ends and cut away half the strands on each end. Twist the two ends together and re-join with a few stitches. Ladder stitch the ends of fabric together and fold back into place. Place this join one third of the way along one side of the cushion and not on a corner.

Complete the cushion by cutting a piece of fabric the same size as the front and lay right sides together. Tack and machine round the cushion leaving a section open in one side. Trim the turnings and clip into the corners to reduce bulk. Oversew the remaining raw edges. Turn to the right side and insert the cushion pad and then ladder stitch together the remaining open edges.

Mitreing corners

Several of the projects in this book call for mitred corners. This is the neatest way of covering a corner. Pull the corner point diagonally and secure to the mounting card with a little glue or, if it is hardboard, use a staple gun. Cut the tail off (A). Fold the corners down and join them together: start at the bottom and work two rows of ladder stitch to reinforce the corner (B).

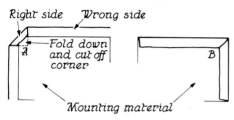

Ladder stitch

Ladder stitch is used throughout this book to stitch two seams together on the right side of the work almost invisibly.

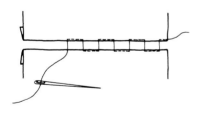

Lacing

Lay the card on to the wrong side of the fabric checking that the grain is parallel to the edge of the card. Mitre the corners. Using crochet cotton or similar strong thread and securing well take the thread from one side of the card to the other, pulling it taut as you go. Fasten off securely. Complete the process by lacing in the other direction.

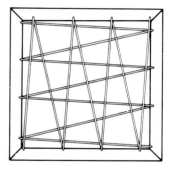

Painting fabrics

Several of the projects in this book incorporate painting areas of the fabric before they are developed with quilting. Quilting and painting combine very successfully.

Fabric paints are easily available from art and craft shops. They are easy to use on most types of fabric, both natural and man-made. All fabrics should be washed and ironed beforehand and must be pressed again afterwards with a hot iron to set the paints and make them fast.

Fabric paints can be used straight from the bottle, mixed with each other or diluted with water. The colours can also be intermixed on the fabric, but unless you specifically want the colours to blend, allow one colour to dry before putting another one on top or beside it. They are really most suitable for small areas.

Apart from painting on with a brush, there are other ways of applying paints to fabric. A sponge is useful for applying larger areas of paint and a stencil brush gives an interesting stippled effect. To keep fabrics in place while working, secure to a working surface with masking tape.

For spraying the paint on to fabric, a mouth diffuser spray, available from art shops, can be used, or a household or garden spray, although with these a minimum of 2 cm ($\frac{3}{4}$ in) is needed in the bottom for it to work. Even a perfume atomiser can be used for small areas. If a lot of spraying is to be incorporated in the work, it may be worth investing in an airbrush.

When spraying, the work has to be in a vertical position. Secure fabric to a board with masking tape or drawing pins and mask the areas not to be sprayed with newspaper. Dilute the fabric paint with water very gradually until it is of milky consistency which flows well.

Having tried fabric paints, one can experiment with other dyes and inks. Even car spray paint can be used on fabrics most successfully.

Tulip evening bag

Materials

50 cm (19 in) cream silk (this is enough for the lining as well)
50 cm (19 in) heavyweight interlining
oddments of silk in blue, grey and cream
50 cm (19 in) peach silk
1 m (1 yd) very fine piping cord
cartridge paper
wadding
interfacing

sewing thread to match for patchwork
sewing thread for making up bag
2 press studs

This bag has been made up in a simple envelope style without any added gussets and is obviously not suitable for carrying many items. However, the same patchwork design can be applied to other clutch-style bags, which could include gussets

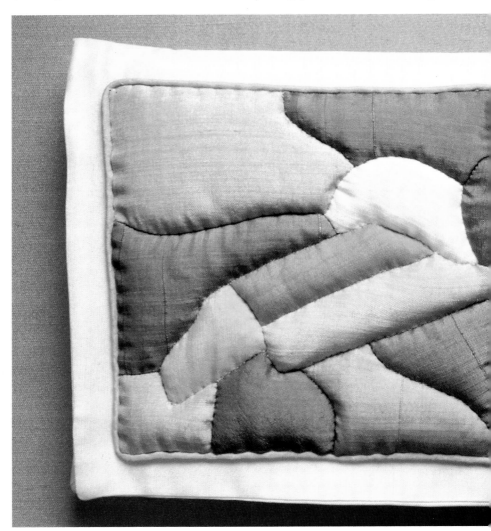

14

and pockets.

Begin with the free patchwork. Trace and enlarge the diagram shown (see page 9) and number the pieces. Draw another identical pattern on to cartridge paper which will be cut up and used as templates. It is advisable to cut only a few at a time and it is very important to be accurate. In order to ensure that the grain goes the same way on each piece, mark an arrow on each template, parallel with the edge. Pin the template to the wrong side of the fabric, with the grain in the same direction as the arrow and cut the fabric out round the template, leaving a seam allowance on all edges of about 6 mm ($\frac{1}{4}$ in). Turn the fabric over the paper template and tack through all layers, clipping the curves so that the turning lies flat.

Begin sewing the patches together.

Bend the shapes and sew them together bit by bit. This will look a little odd while working, but they will lie flat when completed. Cover the other patches in the same way and join them together, following pattern layout. Remove all the templates and tack round the edge of the finished rectangle.

Cut on the cross strips of fabric 4 cm (1½ in) wide, joining where necessary (see page 10). Fold the fabric right side outwards round the cord and stitch close to the cord. Butt the covered cord up to the patchwork and slip stitch into place.

This is now ready to be attached to the flap of the bag.

Cut a piece of silk for the outside of the bag 30 × 47 cm (12 × 18½ in). Check that the top edge is straight and tack in a centre line. Position the patchwork on the fabric.

Cut a piece of wadding slightly smaller than the finished patchwork. Place underneath the silk. Tack through all the layers carefully using matching threads and quilt the patchwork, sinking the stitches into the seams.

Cut interlining and a piece of lining fabric the same size as the main fabric. Lay the main fabric face up on a surface. Place the lining on top and finally the interfacing. Tack all the way round 1 cm (½ in) from the edge, leaving an opening at the opposite end to the patchwork, large enough to turn the work through. Stitch. Trim the interfacing as close to the stitching as possible. Trim corners. Turn the work to the right side and press well. With right sides together, fold up one-third and ladder stitch sides together. Turn out and ladder stitch remaining opening. Press again and attach a press stud to each corner of the flap.

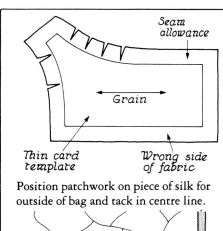

Position patchwork on piece of silk for outside of bag and tack in centre line.

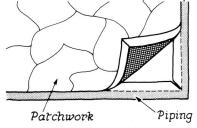

Butt covered cord to patchwork and slip stitch into place.

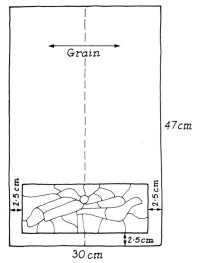

Pin template to wrong side of fabric and cut out, leaving seam allowance. Clip curves.

22·5 x 11·5 cm

Satin cushion

Finished size 35 cm (13½ in) square

Materials

1 m (1 yd) apricot satin
50 cm (19 in) synthetic wadding
50 cm (19 in) fine calico or similar for backing
2 m (2 yd) piping cord
buttonhole twist thread for quilting
sewing thread to match cushion

Trace and enlarge the drawing, bearing in mind that this is just one-quarter of the design.

Cut four 20.5 cm (8 in) squares of satin and join them together to form a large square. If the grain of each fabric is placed in opposite directions, there will be a play of light on the fabric.

Transfer the design on to the fabric using one of the methods described on page 9. Copy the photograph for the layout of the cushion.

Mount the backing fabric on to a frame. Baste the satin, wadding and backing together, working carefully from the centre outwards. After tacking it securely,

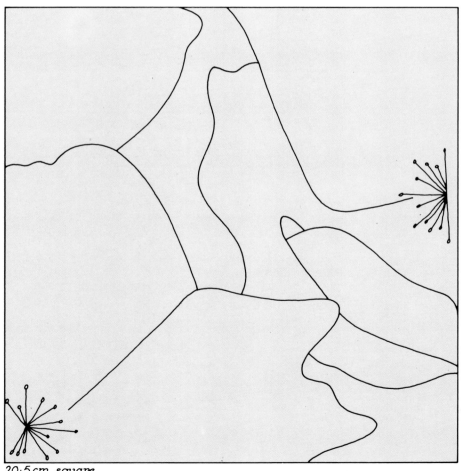

20.5 cm square

quilt along the pattern lines with small regular running or back stitches using the buttonhole twist thread. Work the stamens in stitches of your choice. Remove the tacking threads.

Cut another piece of satin for the back of the cushion, allowing a 1.5 cm ($\frac{5}{8}$ in) seam allowance. Trim the quilted cushion front to within 1.5 cm ($\frac{5}{8}$ in) all round and complete following the instructions for a piped cushion on page 10.

The design for this cushion came from a photograph of a rose. Similar designs can be achieved by cutting two L-shaped pieces of card, and placing them over any photograph or picture to form a window. Move these pieces of card around until you have selected an area that pleases you. The design is now ready for transferring to fabric.

Place a piece of tracing paper over the design and draw in the main lines. This can then be enlarged to the desired size. Draw another three identical designs and place them to form a pattern. This method of designing is suitable for a number of projects.

Cot quilt

Finished size 57 × 75 cm (22½ × 29 in)

Materials

2 m (2 yd) white cotton
50 cm (19 in) blue cotton for sky
50 cm (19 in) green cotton for meadow
50 cm (19 in) pale green cotton for fields
oddment of greeny blue cotton for pond
1 m (1 yd) synthetic wadding
1 m (1 yd) fine calico or similar for backing
stranded embroidery thread
buttonhole twist thread to match for quilting

Trace and enlarge the drawing on to cartridge paper. These pieces can be cut up and used as templates. Cut out sky, hills, meadow and pond using appropriate coloured fabrics. Starting with the sky, tack all pieces together into position, overlapping edges by 1 cm (⅜ in). Cut out rabbits, clouds and trees from white and green fabrics. Cut identical shapes in wadding and tack into position, sandwiching wadding in between. Buttonhole stitch round

the shapes of the hills, rabbits, clouds and trees in matching colours. Mark in the remaining lines from the diagram, with a water-soluble marking pencil. Using stitches of your choice, embroider flowers, rushes, birds, and contour lines, and features on rabbits using two strands of embroidery thread, in position as shown on the diagram. To finish, tack close to all edges and trim. Cut on the cross strips of fabric 2 cm (1 in) wide, enough to go right round the edge of the quilt. Join these pieces of fabric where necessary on the straight grain (see page 10). Place right side of binding to right side of quilt, starting a third of the way along one side and not on a corner, and tack and stitch all round. Cut off any excess binding. Fold binding to wrong side of the quilt, turn under the raw edge and hem.

Alternatively, this could be made up as a wall hanging for a baby's bedroom, by making four loops and attaching them to the back of the hanging.

57 x 75 cm

Greetings cards

Materials

oddments of white satin

wadding

fine calico or similar for backing

green fabric paint for snowdrop

red fabric paint for red campion

thin card

buttonhole twist thread to match

good quality cartridge paper

ruler

Stanley knife

silver pen or dry transfer lettering

masking tape or Sellotape

For the **snowdrop** card, trace and enlarge the flowers on to thin card and carefully cut them out. Lay them on the satin and use a little double-sided Sellotape to keep them in place. Spray the background (see page 11). Leave to dry and then remove the pieces of card. Press well. Assemble the satin, wadding and backing fabric together and tack through the layers. Quilt round the snowdrop flowers and stems with buttonhole twist thread. Trim.

For the card cut a piece of good quality cartridge paper 36 × 25.5 cm (14 × 10 in)

Hot air balloon cushions

Finished size 46 cm (18 in) high × 35 cm (14 in) wide

Materials for Cushion A

50 cm (19 in) cotton lawn in each of two main colours
50 cm (19 in) cotton lawn for back of cushion
50 cm (19 in) synthetic wadding
50 cm (19 in) fine calico to back the wadding
rectangle of calico the size of cushion front plus 5 cm (2 in) all round
sewing thread to match, acrylic stuffing
oddments of cotton lawn for basket

Materials for Cushion B

30 cm (12 in) cotton lawn in four different colours
50 cm (19 in) cotton lawn for back of cushion
oddments of cotton lawn for basket
50 cm (19 in) synthetic wadding
50 cm (19 in) fine calico to back the wadding
rectangle of calico the size of cushion front plus 5 cm (2 in) all round
sewing thread to match, acrylic stuffing

The fabric used for these cushions was cotton lawn. Most fabrics could be used, but avoid one which is too heavy, or which frays easily. *N.B.* No seam allowances are shown on the pattern.

Cushion A: trace and enlarge the design (see page 9). Using the pattern, cut a complete set of card templates of balloon sections and basket, making sure to mark in all letters and notch-mark positions. On the reverse side of the chosen materials lay out and then carefully draw round the templates, allowing space between pieces for seam allowances. Transfer all letter and notch marks to the material. Cut out sections, adding a seam allowance of 5 mm (¼ in) on all edges.

Pin together through the notch marks pieces 1 and 2 using the letters A and B to position correctly against each other. Stitch the pieces together, constantly checking that the pencil lines match. Repeat this process until all the sections have been pieced together. Trim seam allowances except at the outer edges and press lightly. (Do not open seams out flat.)

In order to be able to quilt the front of the balloon right up to the edges, take a rectangle of spare calico which completely covers the front with a margin of 5 cm (2 in) on all edges. Place the front, with right side facing the calico, centrally on to the rectangle and machine baste together, in the outer edge seam allowance. Carefully cut away the calico inside the line of machine basting, thus exposing the front.

Mount the backing fabric on to a frame. Baste the pieced front, wadding and backing together and tack carefully, but be careful not to distort the seams. Using a matching thread, quilt the front, sinking the stitches into the seams. Use the quilting stitches to create the effect of the wicker basket. Once the quilting is completed, remove the machine basting and calico before proceeding.

For the back, mark and cut out the two pieces, adding seam allowances on all edges. Machine stitch the back seam, leaving a central opening for stuffing the cushion through. With right sides together, pin the front to the back and machine stitch. If wished, a second row of stitching can be worked in the seam allowance, close to the first, around the top of the balloon. Turn the cushion the right way out.

Fill the balloon, making sure the basket area is well padded. Then ladder stitch the back opening together. If preferred, a separate cushion pad can be inserted.

Cushion B: trace and enlarge design and make up as for **Cushion A**, but join the pieces, in numerical order, in groups of four to form strips. When all six strips are pieced, join these together and complete as for **Cushion A**.

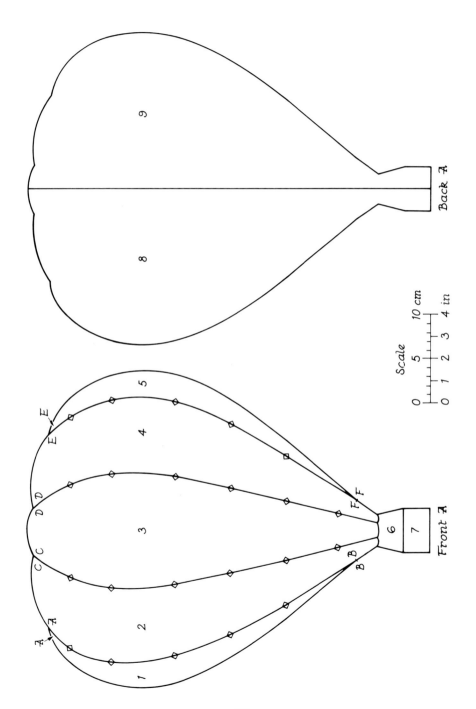

Back A

Front A

Scale

0 — 5 — 10 cm

0 — 1 — 2 — 3 — 4 in

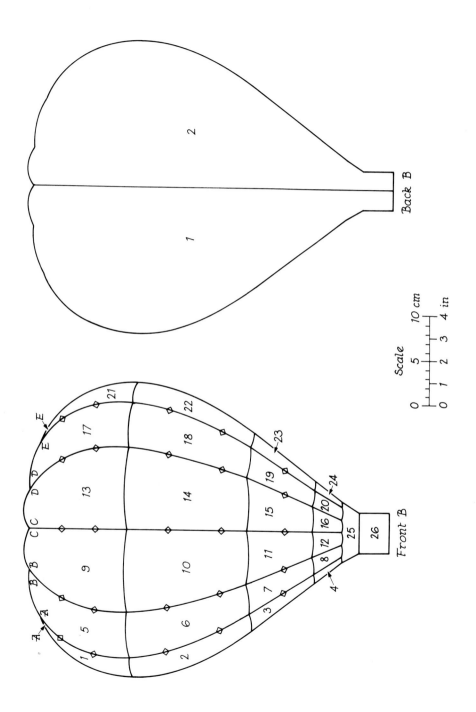

Back B

Front B

Scale

0   5   10 cm

0 1 2 3 4 in

Quilted landscape panel

Finished size 9 × 27 cm (3½ × 10½ in)

Materials
30 cm (12 in) silk
30 cm (12 in) synthetic wadding
30 cm (12 in) fine calico or similar for backing
brown buttonhole silk thread for quilting
mounting card
crochet cotton for lacing
adhesive
water-soluble marking pen
2 small eyelets

The material used for this panel was silk noil, but any closely woven fabric that does not fray easily would be suitable. Trace and enlarge the design shown here (see page 9), or draw the design freely on to the fabric using a water-soluble marking pen. Mount the backing fabric on to a frame. Carefully tack the silk, wadding and backing together. Quilt along the design lines with small regular running or back stitches using the buttonhole silk thread.

Using the mounting card, cut two pieces 27 × 9 cm (10½ × 3½ in). In one of the pieces cut a window 23 × 5 cm (9 × 2 in). (Mounting card is only suitable for small panels. For medium- and larger-size panels hardboard or three-ply would need to be used.)

Cover the piece of card without the window with the finished quilting, trimming the wadding and backing fabric. Centralize the design over the card. Map pins pushed into the card will help to keep the fabric in place while it is being laced. Turn the work over, mitre the corners and lace it as explained on page 11.

Before covering the frame it is advisable to cut four strips of silk on the cross about 4 cm × 5 mm (1½ × ¼ in) and glue them into each corner. This will eliminate any chance of the card being seen, especially if there is a tendency for the fabric to fray.

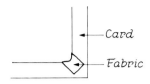

To cover the frame cut a piece of wadding the same size as the frame and put to one side. Cut another piece of silk approximately 14 × 32 cm (5½ × 13 in) and place face downwards with the mount over it. Cut out the inside window from the fabric, leaving 2.5 cm (1 in) all round. Snip into the corners to within 2 mm (1⁄16 in) and glue back the pieces.

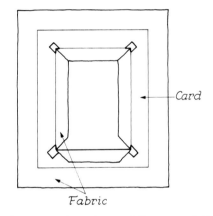

Before inserting the wadding, carefully complete the stitchery to match up with the centre panel. Place the wadding between the mounting card and the top fabric. Place the padded mount over the completed quilting and marry up the edges. Take the surplus fabric to the back of the work, mitre the corners and lace.

To mask the back cut a piece of calico 10 × 28 cm (4 × 11 in), turn under 5 mm (¼ in) all the way round and ladder stitch to the back of the completed work. Two small eyelets can be inserted in the edge of the panel for hanging.

This kind of mount could also be used to frame a mirror.

Glue down the sides of the fabric on to the card, starting where the pieces of card meet. Leave to dry.

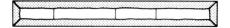

Bend the sides to form the box, making sure that the front and back fit inside the side pieces. Ladder stitch the back to the side piece (see page 11).

Measure the box for the size of the lid. Cut the card for the lid fractionally larger all round than the outside measurements of the box. Cut the fabric to the width of the lid plus 4 cm ($1\frac{1}{2}$ in) for turnings, and for the length, to the depth of the lid plus the height of the back plus 6 cm ($2\frac{1}{4}$ in) for turnings.

Glue down the sides on to the card for the lid and press turnings for the back, tapering slightly towards the bottom. Carefully glue down the side turnings. Trim and glue the corners of the lid fabric and glue down.

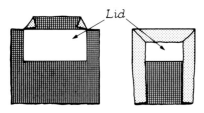

Put glue all over the back of the box, (avoiding the very side edges) and also on the turnings of the back fabric right up to the edge.

Glue the back of the box on to the back fabric, leaving a gap between the card of the lid and the back of the box, so that the lid can be pulled over and closed. Glue turning at the bottom to the inside of the box. Cut a hinge the width of the inside measurement of the box plus turnings if wished and 4 cm ($1\frac{1}{2}$ in) deep. Glue the

hinge inside the box, gluing well down into the gap between the lid and the box, to allow the lid to open, but not to fall back completely.

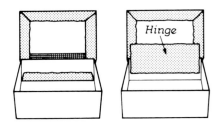

Measure the box for the bottom, cut the card slightly smaller, to allow for its fabric covering, trimming and glueing in the usual way.

Measure the box for the lining pieces, allowing space for the fabric covering and cover all pieces of lining card in the same manner starting with the base.

Measure the sides after the base is fitted, starting with the front and back. Make the lining for the lid small enough to fit inside the lining of the box.

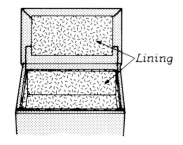

The other boxes are made in the same way. For the small box work the top in English quilting before assembling. The large box uses a patterned fabric and a thick polyester wadding is glued to the lid of the box before assembling as before. The base of the large box will have to be stitched in, as it is too large for the glue to hold in place.

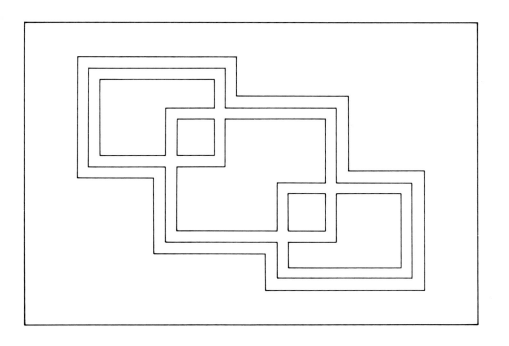

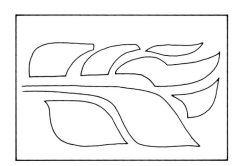

Actual sizes

Quilted folder

Materials

50 cm (19 in) firm cotton fabric
50 cm (19 in) calico for lining
oddment of calico for quilting
wadding
oddment of fine calico for backing
thick card
thin card
buttonhole twist thread for quilting
sewing thread to match
P.V.A. or latex glue
crochet cotton for lacing
ruler
Stanley knife
1 m (1 yd) navy cord

Making a folder is a good way of putting to use all those practice pieces of quilting and they also make very acceptable gifts.

Trace and enlarge the design shown here and transfer to a piece of calico (see page 9). Baste the calico, wadding and backing together and then quilt along the design lines in back and running stitches.

Cut two pieces of thick card 37 × 26 cm (14¾ × 10¼ in). From one piece of card (A) remove a circle with a *Stanley* knife 13.5 cm (5¼ in) in diameter. Smooth the edges off with fine sandpaper.

Cut a piece of fabric the size of the card (A) plus 3 cm (1¼ in) turnings all round. Place the fabric right side down and lay the card (A) on top, making sure that it is on the straight grain of the fabric.

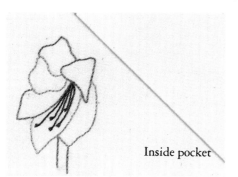

Inside pocket

Cut the fabric in the middle of the circle to within 2 cm (1 in). Clip curves at 1 cm (½ in) intervals all the way round and carefully glue over on to the card.

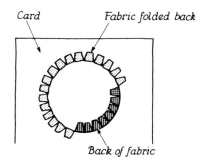

Card   Fabric folded back

Back of fabric

Place the completed quilting in the centre of the circle and glue into place. Mitre the corners and lace or glue the fabric on to the card (see page 11). Cut two pieces of thin card, 3 mm (⅛ in) smaller all round than the outside, to fit the front and back covers as a lining. Cover with calico and lace or glue as before.

For the pocket on the inside front cover, cut a triangular piece of thick card with straight sides measuring 13 cm (5 in). Trace the diagram for the small flower on to a piece of calico and stitch in back stitch. Place the calico over the card allowing turnings of about 2 cm (1 in) and glue the angled edge to the back of the card. Marry up this piece of card with the bottom left hand corner of the front lining. Fold the turnings on to the wrong side of the lining card. Mitre the corner as before and stitch the pocket to the lining. Ladder stitch the lining to the front cover. Complete the back cover as for the front omitting embroidery.

Holes should be made one-third of the way along from each end. Metal eyelets for belts can be inserted according to the instructions or alternatively, a hole can be made with a stiletto, and cord threaded through.

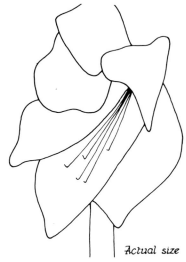

Actual size

Writing paper box

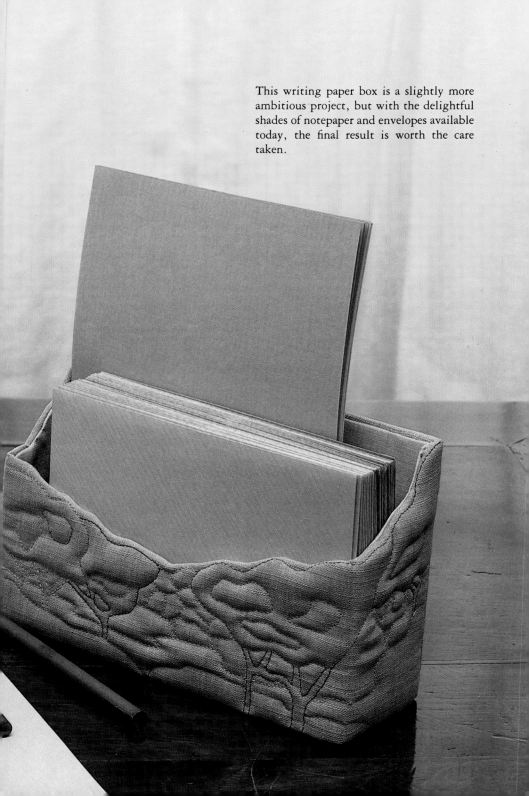

This writing paper box is a slightly more ambitious project, but with the delightful shades of notepaper and envelopes available today, the final result is worth the care taken.

Materials
thick card for outside of box
thin card for lining
50 cm (19 in) cotton fabric for outside of box
50 cm (19 in) lining fabric
synthetic wadding
fine calico or similar for backing
buttonhole twist thread to match for quilting
latex glue
ruler
Stanley knife
sewing thread to match fabric
crochet cotton for lacing

The quilting on the front and sides of this box are worked in one piece. There is no quilting on the back. Trace and enlarge the design and transfer to the fabric (see page 9). Mount the backing fabric on to a frame. Baste the fabric, wadding and backing together, from the centre outwards. Quilt along the lines with running or back stitches using the buttonhole twist thread.

To assemble the box, begin with the base and cut a piece of mounting card 18.5 × 6 cm (7¼ × 2¼ in). Pad one side with felt. Cut a piece of fabric to cover, allowing turnings of 4 cm (1½ in) all round. Mitre the corners and glue or lace the fabric over the card (see page 10). Although the embroidery on the front and sides has been worked in one piece, three pieces of card are cut. For this, enlarge the pattern shape and cut the pieces of card accordingly. If cutting curves for the trees is a little daunting, then just cut it straight across. For the tree tops use a sharp *Stanley* knife and following the outline, cut very lightly at first, then more deeply until the card is cut through. Alternatively, it is just possible to use an old pair of scissors. When the shapes have been cut out, use a piece of fine sandpaper to smooth the edges.

Trim the wadding and backing fabric to the size of the card and allow turnings of

4 cm (1½ in) on the top fabric. Lay the three pieces of card on the reverse side of the fabric with the pieces of card touching. Fold the fabric over the card. To keep the fabric in position while working, push map pins through the fabric into the edge of the card. Mitre the bottom corners. Clip into the curves along the top edge and carefully glue down. Glue the rest of the edges. (See diagram.)

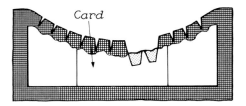

To keep the fabric in place while the glue is drying, place paper clips over the edge.

Cut another piece of mounting card for the back of the box 18.9 × 12 cm (7½ × 4¾ in) and cover as for the base. Fold the sides and join on to the back to form a box. Using ladder stitch, join the back to the side pieces. The sides butt on to the front and back.

Push the sides over the base and pin and ladder stitch all the way round. All the pieces for the lining are constructed separately.

Measure the box for the lining pieces, allowing space for the fabric and cover all pieces of lining card in the same manner, starting with the base. Measure the sides after the base is fitted, starting with the front and back. Cut the top edge of the lining card 3 mm (⅛ in) lower than the box. After making sure that each lining piece fits well, apply adhesive to the wrong side of the lining card and stick into the box and hold with large paper clips until everything is completely dry.

The writing paper box is now ready for the paper and envelopes of your choice.

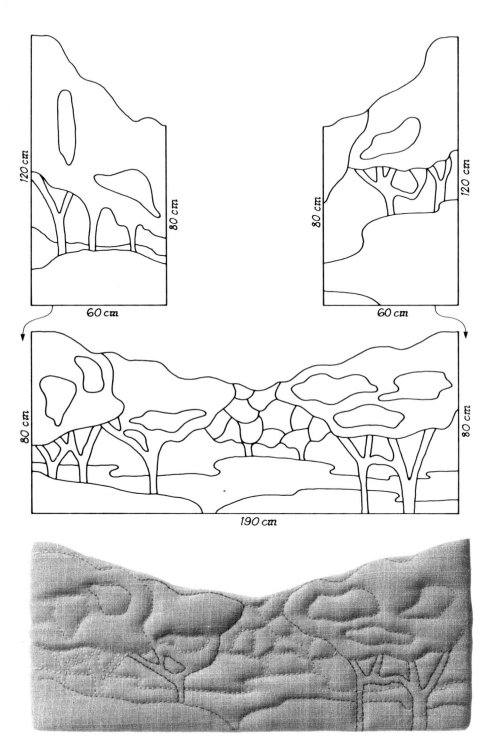

120 cm

80 cm

60 cm

80 cm

120 cm

60 cm

80 cm

80 cm

190 cm

Quilted patchwork bag and purse

Materials

30 cm (12 in) each pink, blue and green cotton
1 m (1 yd) mauve polycotton
sewing thread to match
synthetic wadding
lining material
fine calico or similar for backing
cartridge paper
thin card
1 button mould for covering
1 press stud

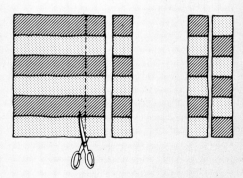

The patchwork used for this bag and purse is an adaptation of a method invented by the Seminole Indians of Florida. They cut brightly coloured fabric strips of varying width, stitched them together, cut them across the seams and re-stitched them to make intricate patterns, which were inserted into their dresses and shirts. For this bag a length of fabric about 50 cm (20 in) square is made up from which the bag and purse is then cut.

To begin, cut strips of the four different coloured fabrics on the straight grain each 3 cm (1¼ in) wide and as long as the fabric will allow. To save time, cut a card strip 3 cm (1¼ in) wide to use as a template.

Taking two colours at a time stitch right sides together taking 5 mm (¼ in) seams, alternating the colours until there are about twenty-four strips, each 2 cm (1 in) wide. This can be done by cutting and re-cutting the long strips and joining them together. At this stage, press the seams to one side. Using the template as a guide, cut the fabric in the opposite direction. The strips are then reversed and sewn together again.

Repeat the process using different colour combinations. To assemble the fabric, intersperse the strips of chequered material with strips of plain fabric the same width. See the photograph for placing of colours. Enlarge the pattern drawings of the bag and purse on to cartridge paper (see page 9). Pin the pattern on the fabric, tack all round the edge and remove pattern. Carefully tack the patchwork, wadding and backing fabric together. Using a matching thread, quilt along the seam lines by hand or machine, sinking the stitches into the seams.

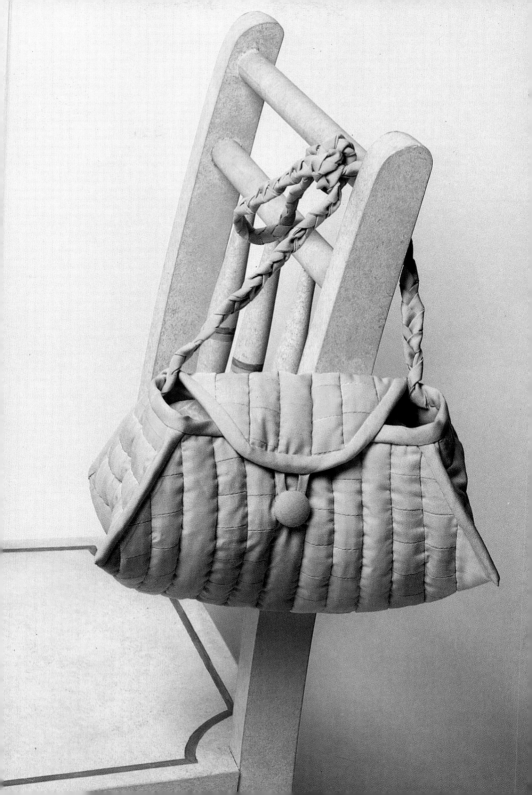

Lay the pattern over the quilting and tack again if necessary, before cutting out the bag. Cut out a lining using the same pattern. Place the lining and bag sections wrong sides together and tack all the way round 5 mm ($\frac{1}{4}$ in) from the edge.

Cut on the cross strips 2 cm (1 in) wide from the lining fabric and join to make a strip of binding long enough to go right round the bag (see page 10).

Fold the bag along the lines shown in the pattern and, placing right side of binding to right side of bag, join A–B first. Tack and stitch. Cut any extra binding off. Turn under raw edge of binding and fold to gusset side. Hem. Starting at C, stitch binding as above along the gusset, then along the front and finishing at other side gusset D.

Before completing the binding, make the strap. Cut three strips on the straight grain in three of the colours used for the bag, each measuring 117 × 4 cm (43 × 1$\frac{1}{2}$ in). Fold right sides together and machine down the long edge and one short end. Pull through to the right side using a small safety-pin and strong thread.

Take two other identical rouleau strips and plait the three together. Neaten the raw edges and trim off the excess. Place the straps at D and C and fasten in with the final hemming.

Complete binding from E–F as above. Before final hemming make a rouleau 6 cm (2$\frac{1}{4}$ in) long for the fastening. Fold in half and attach to the centre of the flap before completing. Cover a button mould with fabric and stitch in place.

The purse is worked in the same way, but the quilting is omitted. Bind the straight edge first, placing right side of binding to right side top edge of bag. Fold A–B with wrong sides together and tack the side seams. With right side of binding to right side of purse, bind all the way round. Attach press stud to purse and flap.

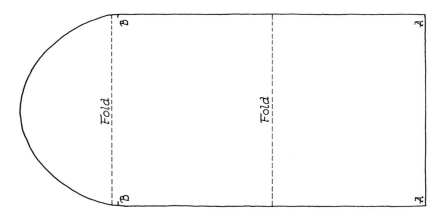

Purse pattern

48

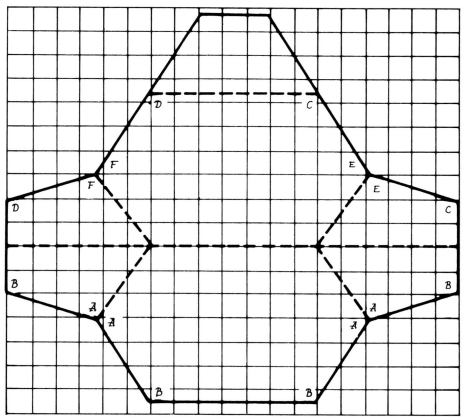

Fold along dotted lines as shown
Each square = 2 cm

Bag pattern

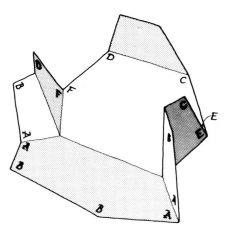

Quilted tree panel

Materials

30 cm (12 in) calico
30 cm (12 in) synthetic wadding
30 cm (12 in) calico or similar for backing
20 cm (8 in) cake board
fabric paints in pink and green
buttonhole twist thread to match for quilting
crochet cotton for lacing
mounting card, thin card
Stanley knife

Fabric paints and quilting are combined in
this circular panel, which uses a cake board
for the base.

Trace and enlarge the design on to a
piece of thin card. Make a stencil by
cutting the large areas out of the card with
a *Stanley* knife. Having decided which
method of fabric painting is to be used (see
page 11), lay the stencil over a piece of
calico and paint or spray the exposed areas.
Remove the stencil and, following the
original drawing, paint in the stems, free-
hand. If you are unsure about this, lightly
draw in the stems first with a very hard
pencil. Leave to dry thoroughly and iron
the calico well to set the paint.

Mount the backing fabric on to a frame.

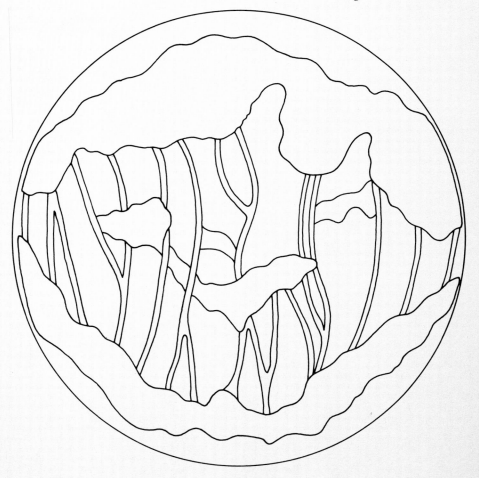

Baste the painted calico, wadding and backing together and quilt following the lines of the stencil. When completed, remove the tacking threads and trim the background fabric and the wadding to the same size as the cake board. Trim the top layer, leaving a margin of about 7 cm ($2\frac{3}{4}$ in) all the way round.

Run a gathering thread about 1 cm ($\frac{1}{2}$ in) from the raw edge (diagram A). Place the quilting over the cake board and position it correctly. Draw the gathering thread up and lace all the way round, pulling tightly until the front is completely smooth (diagram B).

To finish off, cut a piece of card the same diameter as the cake board and cover with a piece of calico using the same method as above. Punch two holes in the card and thread tape through before ladder stitching the back and front together (see page 11). If desired, matching braid can be stitched round the edge of the panel.

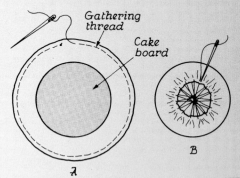

Quilted waistcoat

Materials
bought pattern for sleeveless waistcoat
cream silk, quantity as given on pattern plus
  50 cm (19 in)
synthetic wadding
fine calico or similar for backing
lining fabric—same as for waistcoat
buttonhole twist thread for quilting in three
  shades
matching sewing thread
fabric paint
cartridge paper, masking tape
3 m (3 yd) narrow ribbon

The design for this waistcoat is based on
hedgerows. It can easily be adapted to any
waistcoat pattern. The drawing shown here
is only a guide.

Following pattern layout, place pieces
on to the fabric and tack round on pattern
line. Leaving a border of about 10 cm (4 in)
cut out each piece. This allows for shrinkage during quilting.

Trace and enlarge the design on to
cartridge paper, adjusting to suit the pattern, and transfer to the fabric (see page 9).
Cut a stencil for the painted area from a
second piece of cartridge paper and, using
masking tape, secure to the fabric. Using
fabric paint, spray or paint through the
stencil (see page 11). Leave to dry and press
the fabric pieces well.

Taking each piece in turn, mount the
backing fabric on to a frame. Tack the silk,
wadding and backing together in blocks of
about 5 cm (2 in) from the centre
outwards. Quilt along the pattern lines in
running or back stitch. To give added
emphasis to some of the lower stems, apply
narrow ribbons. A machined zigzag stitch

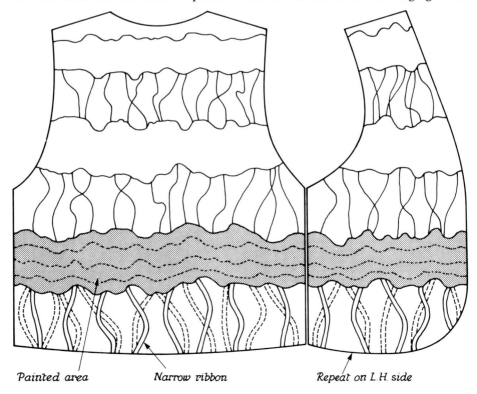

Painted area   Narrow ribbon   Repeat on L.H. side

over them gives even further definition. Work the fronts in the same way.

After the quilting is completed, place the pattern pieces on the fabric again and adjust tacking lines.

Cut out and complete the waistcoat following pattern instructions. If buttons are required, make rouleau loops instead of working buttonholes and insert with the lining. Sew on buttons.

Patchwork and quilted jacket

Materials
bought pattern for jacket
50 cm (19 in) each silver-grey, peach, pale blue
   and navy silk
2 m (2 yd) navy silk (for lining and binding)
silk thread to match
2 m (2 yd) synthetic wadding
2 m (2 yd) fine calico or similar for backing

This jacket was made up using a simple drop-shouldered pattern with no shaping, but any loose jacket pattern would be suitable. Tucked patchwork has been combined with quilting using silk, but any light- or medium-weight fabric could be used.

Cut strips of silk in the four colours in widths of 5 cm (2 in), 6.5 cm (2½ in), 8 cm (3¼ in) and 9.5 cm (3¾ in). This allows 5 mm (¼ in) turnings. Cut the strips in various lengths from 5 cm (2 in) up to 18 cm (7 in) and on some of these, machine pin-tucks 1 cm (½ in) apart varying them in number.

Seam up the patches alternating colours taking 5 mm (¼ in) seams until the lengths are approximately 76 cm (30 in). Press seams open and join the strips until the piece of material is long enough to make the jacket, with a little extra to allow for shrinkage during quilting. Press seams to one side. When seaming strips together, check that no two horizontal seams meet.

Lay the pattern pieces on to the fabric and tack round each piece. Cut out, leaving a margin of about 10 cm (4 in). Taking

each piece in turn tack the patchwork, wadding and backing together and then quilt along the seam lines by hand or machine. To prevent the fabric pulling in opposite directions, always machine from top to bottom.

Place the pattern pieces on the fabric again and adjust pattern lines where necessary. Cut out the jacket and complete following pattern instructions. Cut out the lining in navy silk, stitch seams and slip the lining into place. Cut on the cross strips of fabric 4 cm ($1\frac{1}{2}$ in) wide which will be used to bind the jacket edges and sleeves, and join them where necessary (see page 10). Stitch right side of binding to right side of jacket starting and ending at centre back of neck. Turn binding to wrong side of the jacket, turn under 5 mm ($\frac{1}{4}$ in) and hem all the way round. Bind the edge of the sleeves in the same way.

If buttons are required, make rouleau loops and insert with the lining. Sew on buttons to correspond with the loops.

Logcabin cushion

This cushion combines quilting, patchwork and fabric spraying. The logcabin
design forming the border of the cushion is
a traditional American pattern which nor-
mally uses alternate light and dark tones to
enhance the effect. It is an excellent
method of using up oddments of fabric or,
as shown here, it can be very effective when
worked with shot silk.

17·5 cm **square**

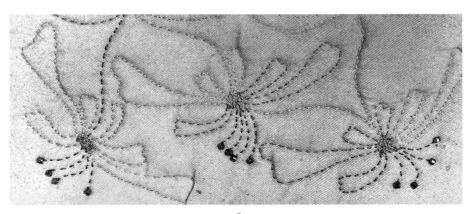

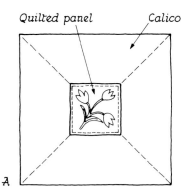

Quilted panel   Calico

A

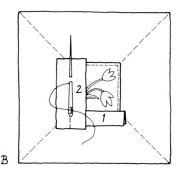

B

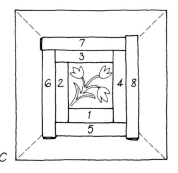

C

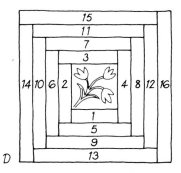

D

Materials
1 m (1 yd) shot silk
oddment of calico for quilting
synthetic wadding
50 cm (19 in) fine calico or similar for backing
buttonhole twist thread to match for quilting
sewing thread to match
2 m (2 yd) piping cord
fabric paint

On a spare piece of calico, spray fabric to tone with the shot silk (see page 9). Trace and enlarge the drawing of honeysuckle and transfer the design to the sprayed calico using one of the methods described on page 11. Tack together the calico, wadding and backing and quilt along the pattern lines with running or back stitch using the buttonhole twist thread. Attach a bead to each stamen and work a cluster of french knots in the centre of each flower. Remove the tacking threads. Trim.

Cut a piece of calico 46 cm (18 in) square and mark diagonally both ways. Apply quilted square to centre of the calico (diagram A). Strips of the shot silk 4 cm (1½ in) wide are then placed round the square in a clockwise direction lapping over each other. The first strip is the length of one side of the central square. Lay it face down on one side of the square with raw edges together. Stitch through all layers on seam line. Fold back and press. Cut the following strip the length of the square plus the width of the previous strip. Lay face down and sew on seam line (diagram B). Continue adding strips until the square is complete (diagram C and D).

Cut another piece of silk for the back of the cushion, allowing a 1.5 cm (⅝ in) seam allowance. Trim the front of the cushion to match and complete following the instructions for a piped cushion on page 10.

Nut and bolt pincushion

Materials
50 cm (19 in) silk
sewing thread to match
chosen embroidery thread
oddment of calico
quilting wool
acrylic stuffing
thin card

This is rather a tricky project to make, and I would not recommend it to a beginner. Instructions are given here for a plain nut and bolt. Work any embroidery if required on to the fabric before starting to assemble. The bolt of the pincushion is made in two pieces and joined together.

Trace and enlarge the drawings shown in the diagram on to thin card, which can then be used as templates. Allowances for seams are not given on the pattern, so allow an extra 1 cm ($\frac{1}{2}$ in) throughout.

Starting with the top of the bolt, cut two pieces A and one piece B from the fabric. With right sides together stitch both pieces A to piece B, leaving side seam open. Make sure top and bottom points on hexagons match up. Snip into corners on each point.

Turn to right side, stuff firmly and ladder stitch opening.

The thread of the bolt is worked next. Cut one piece C, allowing extra fabric to account for shrinkage during quilting. Trace the spiral design onto the fabric. Mount a piece of calico or old sheeting on to a small frame. Lay the fabric on top and using the Italian quilting method (see page 7) stitch along pattern lines. Thread with quilting wool. Remove from frame and trim to size. Stitch a seam 4 cm ($1\frac{1}{2}$ in) down from each end. Cut two pieces D. Embroider one piece if desired. Insert into ends of thread and stitch.

This takes a little time. Clip nearly to line of stitching. Turn to right side. Cut two pieces of thin card using pattern D and insert in to each end of thread. Stuff firmly and ladder stitch opening as you stuff. Sew the un-embroidered end to the underside of the bolt top using ladder stitch and preferably a curved needle.

For the nut, cut one piece B, two pieces E and one piece F. Seam up F on short sides forming a tube. Stitch E to F, top and bottom, clipping curves. Stitch piece B to top of hexagon, clipping into corners. Turn to the right side and ladder stitch remaining seam, stuffing as you go, again making sure that top and bottom hexagon points match up.

The seams can then be accentuated by stitchery.

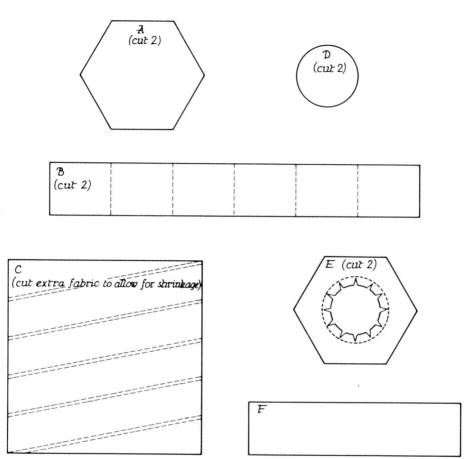

A
(cut 2)

D
(cut 2)

B
(cut 2)

C
(cut extra fabric to allow for shrinkage)

E (cut 2)

F

Seam allowances not included except for centre of 'E'.
Allow 1cm turnings on all sides.

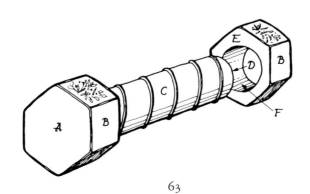

Acknowledgements

My grateful thanks go to Susan Hartree for designing and working the hot air balloon cushions, to Con Meux for the cot quilt and to my mother, Doreen Robson, whose help and encouragement was always there when needed. I would like to thank especially my husband and children for their support throughout the time when I was burning the midnight oil.

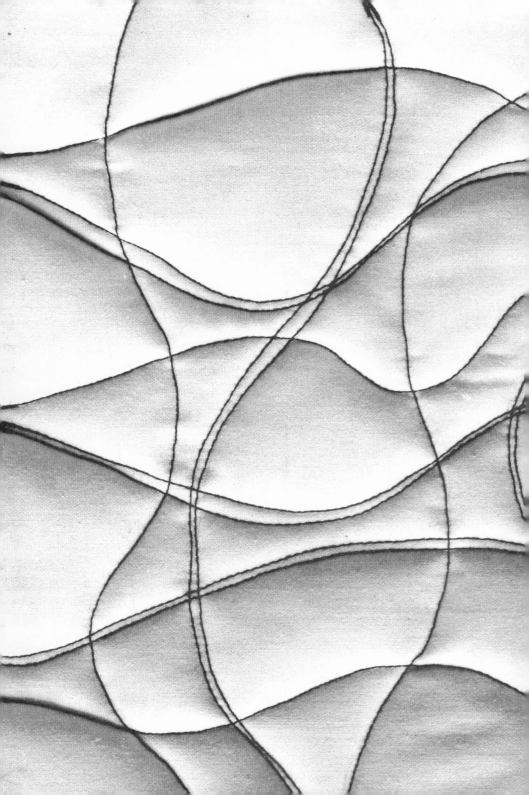